The Story of a Special Day
Volume 63

March 3

62nd day of the year
(63rd in leap years)
303 days remaining
until the end of the year.

by Michael Dobson

Timespinner Press

Copyright Information

Table of Contents

Cover: Original Star Spangled Banner on display at the Smithsonian Institution.

March 3 Quotations

"Leave the beaten track occasionally and dive into the woods. Every time you do so you will find something you have never seen before. Follow it up, explore around it, and before you know it, you will have something to think about to occupy your mind. All really big discoveries are the result of thought."

— Alexander Graham Bell,

born March 3, 1847

"Even if they never got anything for it, it was cheap at that price. Without malice aforethought I had given them the best show that was ever staged in their territory since the landing of the Pilgrims! It was easily worth fifteen million bucks to watch me put the thing over."

— Charles Ponzi, born March 3, 1882

"What we don't know as a nation and as a citizen can kill us."

— Fred W. Friendly, died March 3, 1998

Event of the Day
"The Star-Spangled Banner" Becomes the National Anthem

Although Francis Scott Key wrote "The Star-Spangled Banner" in 1814, about witnessing the bombardment of Fort McHenry during the War of 1812, it wasn't made the United States national anthem until March 3, 1931, when President Herbert Hoover signed a congressional resolution into law.

Although "The Star-Spangled Banner" was a well-known patriotic song soon after it was first published, many other songs were also used officially. For most of the 19th century, "Hail, Columbia" was played at official functions. "My Country, 'Tis of Thee" (sung to the same tune as Britain's "God Save the Queen") was also common.

The Navy adopted "The Star-Spangled Banner" as the official tune for raising the flag in 1889, and President Woodrow Wilson made it official for military occasions in 1916. It was first played at a baseball game during the seventh-inning stretch of the 1918 World Series, but didn't become traditional until World War II.

Believe it or not, the newspaper cartoon strip *Ripley's Believe It or Not!* played an important role when a 1929 strip contained a panel reading, "Believe it or Not, America has no national anthem!" This led John Philip Sousa to publish his opinion that "The Star-Spangled Banner" should receive that honor, and the rest is history.

The actual Star-Spangled Banner was the largest battle flag ever flown at the time, made under government contract at a cost of $405.90. The flag was badly damaged during the battle, and parts of it were cut off as souvenirs, including the 15th star. In 1912, the flag was given to the Smithsonian Institution. It has been restored multiple times, and is now on display in the National Museum of American History in Washington, DC.

Sheet music for "The Star-Spangled Banner," 1862

March 3 Holidays and Celebrations

Hinamatsuri (雛祭り)

The Japanese Doll Festival, or Girls' Day, is held annually on March 3, featuring ornamental dolls placed on a red carpet to represent the Emperor and his family in traditional court dress.

A hina doll display of the Emperor and Empress

Liberation Day (Bulgaria)

Liberation Day, March 3, in Bulgaria celebrates the end of 482 years of Ottoman rule.

Martyr's Day (Malawi)

March 3 in Malawi commemorates the political heroes who gave their lives to fight British colonialism.

Mother's Day (Georgia)

The republic of Georgia celebrates Mother's Day on March 3.

Christian Feast Days

Saints commemorated on March 3 include Cunigunde of Luxembourg and Katharine Drexel.

What Happened on March 3?

1820 CE - Missouri Compromise

On March 3, 1820, the US Congress passed the Missouri Compromise, a deal between pro-slavery and anti-slavery factions. It prohibited slavery in the Louisiana Territory above the parallel 36°30′ except in the proposed new state of Missouri. To balance the addition of Missouri as a slave state, Congress also admitted Maine as a free state, keeping the number of free and slave states equal.

1845 CE - Florida Becomes a State

On March 3, 1845, the former Spanish-owned Florida joined the United States of America as the 27th state.

1861 CE - Russia Frees the Serfs

Tsar Alexander II of Russia emancipated serfs, peasants who were bound to their feudal lords in the Peasant Reform Act of 1861. The

Emancipation Manifesto was issued on March 3, 1861.

1875 CE - *Carmen* Premiers

The opera *Carmen* by Georges Bizet premiers at the Opéra Comique in Paris on March 3, 1875.

1845 CE - Indoor Ice Hockey

The first ever organized indoor game of ice hockey took place in Montreal on March 3, 1875.

1915 CE - NACA Founded

Wanting to improve America's position in the new field of aeronautics, the US Government created the National Advisory Committee for Aeronautics on March 3, 1915. NACA would go on to create several important aviation inventions before its mission was folded into the newly-created National Aeronautics and Space Administration (NASA) in 1958.

1923 CE - *Time* Magazine Starts

The first issue of *Time* magazine, the first weekly news magazine published in the United States, was released on March 3, 1923.

Cover of the first issue of *Time*

1924 CE - The Caliphate Ends

The Caliph of Islam was the religious leader of the Sunni branch of Islam and political ruler of the Muslim world. The caliphate began in 632 CE following the death of the Prophet Muhammad, and lasted 1,400 years until the last Caliph of the Ottoman Dynasty, عبد المجىد الثانى (Abdülmecid II) was deposed and expelled from Turkey on March 3, 1924.

1945 CE - Liberation of Manila

Beginning in late 1944, American and Philippine troops under the command of General Douglas MacArthur began the liberation of the Philippines. The capital city, Manila, fell on March 3, 1945, following a month of terror known as the Manila Massacre, in which over 100,000 civilians were killed, making Manila the second-most destroyed city (after Warsaw) in World War II.

1969 CE - Apollo 9 Launched

Apollo 9, the third manned mission in NASA's Apollo program, tested the Lunar Module and other systems critical to the eventual landing on the Moon. Astronauts James McDivitt, David Scott, and Rusty Schweikart launched on March 3, 1969, and landed ten days later.

Launch of Apollo 9

1991 CE - Rodney King Beaten

On March 3, 1991, Los Angeles police officers arrested construction worker Rodney King after a high-speed chase, and began to beat him, unaware that a resident in a nearby building was videotaping the incident. The acquittal of the police officers involved triggered the 1992 Los Angeles riots, in which 53 people were killed and over 2,000 injured. Later, two of the police officers were tried in federal court and were convicted.

1991 CE - Latvia and Estonia Become Independent

In referenda held in the two Baltic nations of Latvia and Estonia on March 3, 1991, the population voted for independence from the Soviet Union by substantial margins.

2005 CE - Round-the-World Without Refueling

Taking off on February 28, 2005, and landing 67 hours later on March 3, pilot and adventurer Steve Fossett made the first solo nonstop unrefueled fixed-wing aircraft flight around the world in the specially designed Virgin Atlantic GlobalFlyer.

Steve Fossett in the Virgin Atlantic GlobalFlyer

Who Was Born on March 3?

The abbreviation "O.S." on some dates refers to the fact that the Russian Empire did not switch from the Julian to the Gregorian calendar at the same time as the rest of Europe, and therefore some figures have two dates for their birth or death.

People whose original names are not in the Western alphabet have their native names in the appropriate script shown in parenthesis.

Acting and Modeling

Jessica Biel (March 3, 1982 —)

Actress Jessica Biel first became known for her role in the television series *7th Heaven* and subsequently starred in a number of movies.

David Faustino (March 3, 1974 —)

David Faustino is best known for playing son Bud Bundy on the television sitcom *Married...With Children.*

Victoria Zdrok (March 3, 1973 —)

Model and actress Victoria Zdrok was the *Playboy* Playmate of the Month for October 1994, the *Penthouse* Pet of the Month for June 2002, and *Penthouse* Pet of the Year for 2004. She holds a JD from Villanova University and a PhD in Clinical Psychology from Drexel University.

Laura Harring (March 3, 1964 —)

Miss USA for 1985, Laura Harring also played Rita in the 2001 film *Mulholland Drive.*

Ira Glass (March 3, 1959 —)

Ira Glass is the host and producer of the long-running public radio and television series *This American Life.*

Miranda Richardson (March 3, 1958 —)

Actress Miranda Richardson has won two Golden Globes and received two Academy Award nominations during her career.

Darnell Williams (March 3, 1955 —)

Soap opera star Darnell Williams won two Daytime Emmy Awards for playing Jesse Hubbard on the ABC series *All My Children.*

Tim Kazurinsky (March 3, 1950 —)

A cast member on *Saturday Night Live* from 1981 to 1984, Tim Kazurinsky also acted in the *Police Academy* film series.

Gloria Hendry (March 3, 1949 —)

Actress Gloria Hendry played the "Bond girl" in *Live and Let Die,* and starred in several 1970s blaxploitation films.

George Miller (March 3, 1945 —)

Australian film director George Miller is best known for his *Mad Max* trilogy, and also directed *Happy Feet* and the *Babe* series.

Bobby Driscoll (March 3, 1937 — March 30, 1968)

Child actor Bobby Driscoll starred in Disney films including *Song of the South* and *Treasure Island,* and served as the animation model and voice for the title role in *Peter Pan.* He received an Academy Juvenile Award in 1950. He died in poverty after a prison term for drug abuse.

Barney Martin (March 3, 1923 — March 21, 2005)

Veteran actor Barney Martin is best remembered for playing the father of Jerry Seinfeld on the television sitcom *Seinfeld.*

James Doohan (March 3, 1920 — July 20, 2005)

Canadian actor James Doohan is best known for playing chief engineer of the starship *Enterprise* in the original *Star Trek* series and numerous movies.

James Doohan as "Scotty" in *Star Trek*

Jean Harlow (March 3, 1911— June 7, 1937)

Jean Harlow was named one of the greatest movie stars of all time by the American Film

21

Institute. She was considered a sex symbol, and was nicknamed "Blonde Bombshell" and "Platinum Blonde." She died at the age of 26.

Jean Harlow

Aviation

Lincoln J. Beachey (March 3, 1887 — March 14, 1915)

Pioneer aviator Lincoln J. Beachey was known in his day as "The World's Greatest Aviator." He was the first aviator to fly inverted, the first to complete an inside loop, and the first to fly inside a building. He was also famous for racing automobile legend Barney Oldfield, pitting his biplane against Oldfield's car in numerous exhibitions.

Lincoln Beachey

Art and Literature

Glen E. Friedman (March 3, 1962 —)

Photographer Glen E. Friedman was named "one of the greats of his generation" by the Washington *Post*. His iconic photography of skateboarders and musicians is in the collection of numerous major museums.

James Merrill (March 3, 1926 — February 6, 1995)

American poet James Merrill won the 1977 Pulitzer Prize for his work *Divine Comedies*.

Ronald Searle (March 3, 1920 — December 30, 2011)

Satirical cartoonist Ronald Searle received numerous awards for his work and is considered an influence on American artists including Matt Groening *(The Simpsons)* and the animators of Disney's *101 Dalmatians*.

Beatrice Wood (March 3, 1893— March 12, 1998)

Artist and potter Beatrice Wood was known as the "Mama of Dada" for her art, and was a partial inspiration for the character of Rose in James Cameron's 1997 film *Titanic*.

William Godwin (March 3, 1756 — April 7, 1836)

William Godwin's prominence as a political philosopher came from his advocacy of utilitarianism and anarchy. He is perhaps better known as the father of Mary Godwin (Wollstonecraft), who married the poet Percy Bysshe Shelly and wrote the novel *Frankenstein*.

Business and Industry

Jamsetji Tata (જમશેત્જી નુસ્સેર્વાનજી ટાટા)
(March 3, 1839 — May 19, 1904)

Indian industrialist Jamsetji Tata founded the Tata Group, India's biggest conglomerate, and is known as the "father of Indian industry."

George Pullman (March 3, 1831 — October 19, 1897)

George Pullman is known as the inventor of the Pullman sleeping car for railroads, and for violently suppressing striking workers in the 1894 Pullman strike, a key event in labor history.

George Pullman

Crime

Charles Ponzi (March 3, 1882 — January 18, 1949)

Italian con artist Charles Ponzi became known for his 1920 swindle in which he paid early investors with the money from later investors, giving the impression of great returns. This swindle cost investors over $20 million ($225 million in 2011), and brought down five banks. This type of scam is now known as a "Ponzi scheme," although he was not the first to use it.

Fashion and Design

Perry Ellis (March 3, 1940 — May 30, 1986)

Menswear designer Perry Ellis won eight Coty Awards in his long career.

Lee Radziwill (March 3, 1933 —)

Younger sister of former First Lady Jacqueline Kennedy Onassis, Lee Radziwill was known as an accomplished interior designer and as a public relations executive for Giorgio Armani. She received the French Legion of Honor in 2008.

Music

Tone Lōc (March 3, 1966 —)

Rapper Tone Lōc is best known for his hits "Wild Thing" and "Funky Cold Medina."

Jennifer Warnes (March 3, 1947 —)

Singer and songwriter Jennifer Warnes won three Academy Awards for Best Original Song. Her hits include "Up Where We Belong" from *An Officer and a Gentleman* and "(I've Had) The Time of My Life" from *Dirty Dancing*.

Doc Watson (March 3, 1923— May 29, 2012)

Bluegrass and folk guitarist and songwriter Doc Watson won seven Grammy awards and a Grammy Lifetime Achievement Award for his extensive body of work.

Doc Watson

Politics and Military

Tomiichi Murayama (村山 富市) (March 3, 1924 —)

Former Prime Minister of Japan Tomiichi Murayama is best known outside Japan for his 1995 speech apologizing for Japanese atrocities committed during World War II.

Matthew Ridgway (March 3, 1895— July 26, 1993)

General Matthew Ridgway commanded the 82nd Airborne in the 1943 invasion of Sicily and the 8th US Army in the Korean War. He replaced Douglas MacArthur as commanding general in Korea and as military governor of Japan. He was known as "Old Iron Tits" for his habit of wearing hand grenades at chest level.

Madeleine de Verchères (March 3, 1678 — August 8, 1747)

Canadian heroine Madeleine de Verchères is famous for her role in stopping an Iroquois attack on Fort Verchères when she was 14 years old.

João II, King of Portugal (March 3, 1455 — October 25, 1495)

Known as the "Perfect Prince," João II of Portugal turned his bankrupt kingdom around by his policies of encouraging Atlantic and African exploration. He claimed Columbus's discoveries for Portugal, resulting in the Treaty of Tordesillas, which divided the newly discovered lands between Portugal and Spain.

João II, King of Portugal

Science and Technology

Alexander Graham Bell

Alexander Graham Bell (March 3, 1847 — August 2, 1922)

Inventor of the first practical telephone, Alexander Graham Bell also did groundbreaking work in many other fields, including the invention of the metal detector, the hydrofoil, and numerous advances in early aviation. He helped found the Bell Telephone Company (later AT&T). He was also well known for his work with the deaf, and in that work tutored a young Helen Keller.

Georg Cantor (March 3[O.S. February 19], 1845 — January 6, 1918)

German mathematician Georg Cantor is known as the inventor of set theory, one of the fundamental theories of mathematics.

Sports

Santonio Holmes (March 3, 1984 —)

New York Jets wide receiver Santonio Holmes was named MVP of Super Bowl XLIII.

Brian Leetch (March 3, 1968 —)

Ice hockey player Brian Leetch won numerous honors, including the Norris Trophy, the Conn Smith Trophy, and the Calder Trophy. He is a member of the Hockey Hall of Fame.

Herschel Walker (March 3, 1962 —)

Winner of the 1982 Heisman Trophy, Herschel Walker played for the Dallas Cowboys, Minnesota Vikings, Philadelphia Eagles, and the New York Giants. He was inducted into the College Football Hall of Fame in 1999.

Jackie Joyner-Kersee (March 3, 1962 —)

Named the Greatest Female Athlete of the 20th Century by *Sports Illustrated,* Jackie Joyner-Kersee won three gold, one silver, and two bronze Olympic medals in the women's heptathlon and the women's long jump.

Who Died on March 3?

Art and Literature

Hergé (May 22, 1907 — March 3, 1983)

Belgian artist and writer Hergé was best known for his comic book series *The Adventures of Tintin*. A national hero in Belgium, the Hergé Museum is devoted to his work.

Business

George Gilman (1826 — March 3, 1901)

Businessman George Gilman founded The Great Atlantic and Pacific Tea Company, better known as A&P, which became the world's largest retailer, with over 16,000 stores at its height.

Movies and Television

Ralph McQuarrie (June 13, 1929 — March 3, 2012)

Designer and illustrator Ralph McQuarrie created the visual design for the original *Star Wars* trilogy, *E.T. the Extra-Terrestrial,* and *Cocoon,* winning an Academy Award for the latter.

Horst Buchholz (December 4, 1933 — March 3, 2003)

German actor Horst Buchholz played Chico in *The Magnificent Seven*, as well as acting in over 60 other films.

Fred Friendly (October 30, 1915 — March 3, 1998)

Fred Friendly was president of CBS News, and co-creator (with Edward R. Murrow) of the documentary series *See It Now.* He also originated the concept of public broadcasting and played a major role in establishing the Public Broadcasting Service (PBS).

Danny Kaye (January 18, 1913 — March 3, 1987)

Actor, singer, dancer, and comedian Danny Kaye starred in 17 movies, had a successful TV show, and served as UNICEF's first ambassador-at-large. He received the French Legion of Honor in 1986 for his philanthropic work.

Danny Kaye entertaining the troops

William Frawley (February 26, 1887 — March 3, 1966)

Featured in over 100 films, William Frawley is best known for playing landlord Fred Mertz in the TV sitcom *I Love Lucy*.

Lou Costello (March 6, 1906 — March 3, 1959)

Chubby comedian Lou Costello was best known as half of the comedy duo Abbott and Costello, and for his trademark phrase, "Hey, Abbott!"

Lou Costello (left) with Hillary Brooke in *Africa Screams*

Music and Dance

Carlos Montoya (December 13, 1903 — March 3, 1993)

Flamenco guitarist Carlos Montoya helped popularize the musical genre worldwide.

Arthur Murray (April 4, 1895 — March 3, 1991)

Dance instructor Arthur Murray developed a national chain of dance studios, in which he taught the leading figures of the day. He was inducted into the National Museum of Dance's Hallof Fame in 2007.

Politics

Aurangzeb (November 4, 1618 — March 3, 1707)

A descendant of Genghis Khan, Aurangzeb was the sixth Mughal Emperor, ruler of most of the Indian subcontinent. He expanded his empire to rule over 100 million subjects.

Science and Medicine

Albert Sabin (August 26, 1906 — March 3, 1993)

American medical researcher Albert Sabin is best known for the development of the oral polio vaccine in the 1950s.

Robert Hooke (July 28 [O.S. July 18] 1635 — March 3, 1703)

Scientist Robert Hooke worked in a variety of disciplines, but is best known for Hooke's Law of Elasticity ($F = -kx$).

Sports

James J. Jeffries (April 15, 1875 — March 3, 1953)

Professional boxer James J. Jeffries won the World Heavyweight Championship in 1899. After his retirement in 1905, he made a comeback in "The Fight of the Century" against black champion Jack Johnson, but was defeated by TKO in the 15th round.

Ned Williamson (October 24, 1857 — March 3, 1894)

Baseball player Ned Williamson held the home run record until 1919, until it was topped by Babe Ruth.

Ned Williamson

The month of March, from the illuminated manuscript
Les Très Riches Heures du duc de Berry

March: The Story of a Month

The Third Month

In ancient Rome, March was the first month of the year. As the first month of spring, in the Mediterranean climate it marked the beginning of the military campaign season. That's why March (Martius) is named in honor of Mars, the Roman god of war.

Although the first month of the year was moved back to January sometime during the transition of Rome from a kingdom to a republic (historians differ), March was the first month of the year in Russia until the end of the 15th Century, and is the first month of the year in many other cultures and religions.

In the northern hemisphere, March 1 marks the beginning of meteorological spring. In the southern hemisphere, March is the equivalent of September, making southern hemisphere March the beginning of autumn.

March is one of the seven months that have 31 days in it. March starts on the same day of the week as November every year, and except for leap years starts on the same day as February. March starts on the same day of the week as the previous June except for leap years, and in leap years starts on the same day as the previous September and December.

March in Other Cultures

In Finland, March is called *maaliskuu* (earthy month). In Ukraine, it's *березень* (birch tree). Other names for March include *Lentmonat* (Saxon), *Hyld-monath* (Angles), and *sušec* (Slovene).

March Symbols

Birthstones: Aquamarine and bloodstone, both representing courage.

Aquamarine

Birth Flowers
Daffodils

Daffodils in Bagatelle Park, Paris, France

March Events

Honorary months: Presidents, Congresses, and nations around the world issue proclamations recognizing particular months to honor certain causes. These events generally fall in March. (All US unless otherwise noted.)

- National Nutrition Month

- American Red Cross Month

- Women's History Month (celebrated in Canada during October)

- Irish-American Heritage Month

- Colorectal Cancer Awareness Month

- Fire Prevention Month (The Philippines)

Women's Suffrage picket line, 1917

"March Madness": (United States) The NCAA Men's Division I Basketball Championship, popularly known as "March Madness" or the "Big Dance," is a single-elimination tournament to establish the champion college basketball team.

Multi-day events: Some March events span multiple days.

- **Nineteen Day Fast:** (Bahá'í Faith) March 2 through March 20

Movable events: Some events change dates from year to year.

- **Mardi Gras:** French for "Fat Tuesday," this celebration takes place the day before Ash Wednesday, the beginning of the Lenten season. The New Orleans Mardi Gras celebration is perhaps the most famous, but Mardi Gras and the Carnival season (between Ephiphany and Ash Wednesday) are celebrated in many areas with large Catholic populations. Mardi Gras can take place anywhere from February 3 to March 9 in regular years, and from February 4 to March 9 in leap years.

- **Casimir Pulaski Day:** (Illinois) The first Monday in March is observed as a holiday in Illinois, in memory of the Revolutionary War cavalry officer born in Poland. Dates range from March 1 to March 7.

Mardi Gras Night Parade, New Orleans, 2012

March Zodiac Signs

From the perspective of someone on Earth, the Sun appears to move through the sky throughout the year, along a path astronomers call the ecliptic plane. The ecliptic plane is divided into twelve constellations, known as the zodiac, based on traditionally observed patterns of stars. On your birthday, you can't see your constellation, because it's part of the daytime sky.

The zodiac was first developed by Babylonian astronomers about 2,500 years ago. Because they were unaware that the Earth wobbles like a spinning top (a motion known as *precession*), they didn't make allowance for the fact that the Sun's path through the zodiac changes over time.

That means there are now two sets of dates for your birth sign. The *tropical dates* are the original Babylonian dates; the *siderial dates* tell you where the Sun actually appears as it moves along its annual path.

Zodiac signs in March are Aquarius and Pisces.

Aquarius

Tropical January 20 to February 19

Siderial February 12 to March 8 (March 9 in leap years)

Aquarius is one of the oldest recognized constellations, originally representing the Babylonian god Ea. In Latin, Aquarius means "water-carrier," represented in its symbol. In Greek mythology, Aquarius is sometimes associated with Deucalion, who survived a world-cleansing flood. In Chinese astronomy, it is known as the Black Tortoise of the North (北方玄武, Běi Fāng Xuán Wǔ).

In astrology, Aquarius is considered to be masculine and extroverted, and despite the name is an air sign. Aquarians are supposed to be philanthropical, inventive, and individualistic.

Pisces

Tropical February 20 to March 20

Siderial March 15 to April 14

In the Roman legend of Venus and her son Cupid, they escaped the clutches of Typhon, known as the "father of all monsters," by transforming into fish and tying themselves together with rope. That's why the name Pisces is plural for fish. The constellation appears as a somewhat ragged "V" shape, representing the rope, with the "fish" located at the two rope ends.

In astrology, Pisces is a water sign, compatible with the other water signs Cancer and Scorpio, as well as with the earth signs Taurus, Virgo, and Capricorn. Pisceans are supposed to be imaginative, compassionate, unworldly, secretive, and escapist.

What Day of the Week?

On what day of the week does March 3 fall?

Unfortunately, this isn't an easy question. Because the calendar year is 365 days long (366 in leap years), it doesn't divide evenly by the seven days of the week.

Also, the Earth goes around the Sun in about 365-1/4 days, so a calendar tends to drift over time. That's why the same date falls on different weekdays in different years.

This is made even more complicated by a change in calendars that took place in 1582. Our modern calendar has its roots in ancient Rome, in a calendar reform conducted by Julius Caesar. Caesar commissioned mathematicians to attack the problem, and came up with the idea of *leap years*, and thus standardized the calendar for centuries to come. This was called the *Julian calendar.*

Over time, however, the small errors in Caesar's calculation compounded. That's why Pope Gregory XIII commissioned the *Gregorian calendar*, used in most of the world today. Some countries converted in 1582, when the calendar was first developed; some converted later; other still haven't changed.

Gregorian and Julian aren't the only types of calendars. The Hebrew year, the Islamic year, and many other calendars are used in different parts of the world and among different people.

You can convert Gregorian dates to other calendars, including the Hebrew calendar, the Islamic calendar, and even the Mayan calendar by visiting the Fourmilab Calendar Converter at http://www.fourmilab.ch/documents/calendar/.

A 50-year brass perpetual calendar.

Copyright, Credit, and Contact

Follow Us

Our blog Dobson's Improbable History features short articles on events and people associated with each day, and updates several times each week. Get the latest on Twitter @SidewiseThinker.

Sources and Art Credits

All art and photographs are either in the public domain or used under a Creative Commons license. Attribution is provided where requested by the copyright owner or when of historical significance, listed below.

- The cover image of the Star-Spangled Banner on display at the Smithsonian's National Museum of American History is from the Smithsonian Institution Archives and is not covered by copyright.

- The sheet music for "The Star-Spangled Banner" comes from the Project Gutenberg archives. The copyright is expired, and the image is in the public domain.

- The photograph of the top platform of a hina doll set was taken by Nesnad and is licensed under the Creative Commons Attribution-Share Alike 3.0 Unported license.

- The cover of the first issue of *Time* is in the public domain because its copyright was not renewed.

- The photograph of the launch of Apollo 9 and the photograph of Steve Fossett in the Virgin Atlantic GlobalFlyer were taken by NASA and are in the public domain.

- The publicity photographs of James Doohan and Jean Harlow are in the public domain.

- The 1913 photograph of Lincoln Beachey is from the Library of Congress Prints and Photographs Division and is in the public domain.

- The photograph of George Pullman is in the public domain because its copyright has expired.

- The photograph of Doc Watson comes from Doc Watson and is licensed under the Creative Commons Attribution 2.0 Generic license.

- The portrait of João II, King of Portugal, is in the public domain because its copyright is expired. The artist is unknown.

- The 1892 photograph of Alexander Graham Bell making the first New York to Chicago telephone call is in the public domain. It is part of the Gilbert H.

Gosvenor Collection in the Library of Congress' Prints and Photographs Division.

- The photograph of Danny Kaye entertaining the 5th Marine Division, Japan, 1945, was taken by Pfc. H. J. Grimm, and is in the collection of the National Archives and Records Administration. It is in the public domain.

- The screenshot of Lou Costello from *Africa Screams* is in the public domain because its copyright was not renewed.

- The Goodwin & Company 1887 baseball card of Ned Williamson is in the public domain because its copyright has expired.

- The illustration of the month of March is from the French Gothic illuminated manuscript *Les Très Riches Heures du duc de Berry* by the Limbourg Brothers, Jean Colombe, and an intermediate painter whose name is lost to history.

- The photograph of aquamarine has been released into the public domain.

- The photograph of daffodils is by Myrabella, and is licensed under the Creative Commons Attribution-Share Alike 3.0 Unported license.

- The 1917 Women's Suffrage demonstration comes from the Library of Congress, Prints and Photographs Division, LC-USZ62-31799 DLC

- The photograph of the 2012 Mardi Gras Night Parade was taken by Mills Baker, licensed under the Creative Commons Attribution 2.0 Generic License.

- The photograph of *hanácké kraslice*, a traditional way of decorating Easter eggs with straw, was taken on an exhibition of egg decorating in Bělkovice-Lašťany in the Czech Republic, and is in the public domain.

- The 50-year perpetual calendar photograph is in the public domain.